Gospel Light's

SONFORCE KIDS

SPECIAL AGENTS

On a Mission for God DECODING JOSHUA 1:9

Bible Story Center Guide
with Reproducible Pages

Preteen · Ages 10 to 12 · Grades 5 and 6

HOW TO MAKE CLEAN COPIES FROM THIS BOOK

You may make copies of portions of this book with a clean conscience if

- you (or someone in your organization) are the original purchaser;
- you are using the copies you make for a noncommercial purpose (such as teaching or promoting your ministry) within your church or organization;
- you follow the instructions provided in this book.

However, it is ILLEGAL for you to make copies if

- you are using the material to promote, advertise or sell a product or service other than for ministry fund-raising;
- you are using the material in or on a product for sale; or
- you or your organization are not the original purchaser of this book.

By following these guidelines you help us keep our products affordable.

Thank you, *Gospel Light*

Gospel Light Vacation Bible School

Senior Managing Editor, Sheryl Haystead • **Senior Editor,** Heather Kempton Wahl
Editorial Team, Karen McGraw, Becky Garcia
Contributing Editors, Ninalu Bovensiep, Kim Fiano, Denise Hatcher, Christy Weir, Tammy Wise-DiPerna
Art Directors, Lori Hamilton, Samantha A. Hsu, Lenndy McCullough

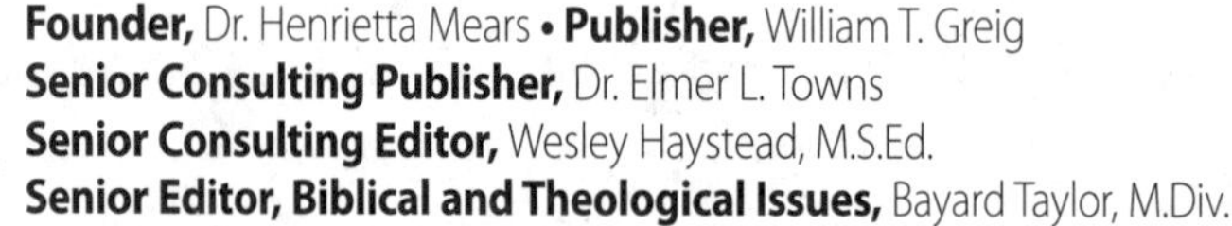

Founder, Dr. Henrietta Mears • **Publisher,** William T. Greig
Senior Consulting Publisher, Dr. Elmer L. Towns
Senior Consulting Editor, Wesley Haystead, M.S.Ed.
Senior Editor, Biblical and Theological Issues, Bayard Taylor, M.Div.

Contents

Teaching Helps

Evangelism Opportunity

Focus on Evangelism

This symbol highlights portions of the lessons that provide special opportunities to explain the gospel message to children. Look for this symbol in the Tell the Story section of each lesson.

Sessions

Reproducible Pages

Course Description

SonForce Kids Special Agents

Invite your students to join SonForce Kids—God's courageous team of disciples standing side-by-side to serve Him. As SonForce special agents, they will follow in the words of Joshua 1:9: *Be strong and courageous. Do not be terrified; do not be discouraged, for the Lord your God will be with you wherever you go.*

The SonForce Kids headquarters is located on a satellite orbiting high above the earth. In this hi-tech command center, SonForce agents gather to prepare for their five Daily Missions: Trust! Unite! Train! Follow! Lead! Throughout VBS, your students will have the opportunity to grow in their understanding of what it means to serve God with courage as they advance from Level 1 to Level 5 agents.

From the courage shown by baby Moses' family, Level 1 agents will learn to **TRUST in God's Plans**. Following Esther's example, Level 2 agents will be encouraged to **UNITE with God's People**. To help them make wise choices like Daniel did, Level 3 agents will learn to **TRAIN for God's Service**. Just as Jeremiah obeyed God even when it was difficult, Level 4 agents will learn to **FOLLOW in God's Path**. Finally, like Joshua and Caleb, Level 5 agents will get ready to **LEAD Others to God's Promises**.

So get ready for an out-of-this-world adventure. SonForce Kids—courageous kids on a mission for God!

Supply List

General Supplies

- ◇ Bible Story Posters for Sessions 1-5 from *Elementary Teaching Resources*
- ◇ *SonForce Kids CD* and player
- ◇ Daily Missions stickers
- ◇ colored markers
- ◇ masking tape
- ◇ ruler
- ◇ measuring stick
- ◇ pencils
- ◇ Post-it Notes
- ◇ scissors
- ◇ paper cutter

For each student—

- ◇ Bible
- ◇ *SFA Manual*

Session 1

Guess the Question

- ◇ Agent Identification Cards (p. 40)

Back It Up

- ◇ Back It Up Cards (p. 41)

Apply the Story

- ◇ small basket

Session 2

Rocket Races

- ◇ People Cards (p. 42)

For each team of four to six students

- ◇ two sheets of construction paper

Zig and Zag

- ◇ Zigzag Verse Cards (p. 43)

Session 3

Agents in Training

- ◇ paper lunch bag
- ◇ large sheets of paper

Tic-Tac-Toe Training

- ◇ Tic-Tac-Toe Cards (p. 44)
- ◇ scrap paper

Apply the Story

- ◇ sheet of paper
- ◇ clipboard

Session 4

Hoverboard Hustle

- ◇ Command Cards (p. 45)
- ◇ two skateboards

Around and Around

- ◇ Around and Around Code (p. 46)
- ◇ transparent tape

For each student—

- ◇ toilet-paper tube, 5 3/8 inches (13.4 cm) in circumference

Apply the Story

- ◇ length of butcher paper

Session 5

Promise Plates

- ◇ Promise Cards (p. 47)
- ◇ paper plates
- ◇ beanbag

Strip Slidin' Away

- ◇ Slidin' Strips and Cards (p. 48)
- ◇ card stock
- ◇ transparent tape

Optional—

- ◇ craft knife and cutting mat

Decorating Your Center

Trans Port

A few simple decorations can transform an ordinary classroom into part of the SonForce Kids satellite headquarters. Use a variety of real items and/or painted backdrops. *Reproducible Resources* contains patterns and more detailed instructions. For additional information, see the decorating segment of the *Preview DVD*.

Turn your Bible Story Center into the Trans Port, where SonForce agents are transported to Bible times to witness real events from the Bible. Enlarge the Palace Backdrop and Desert/Nile Backdrop Patterns found in *Reproducible Resources* onto butcher paper, paint and attach to adjoining walls.

Bring your backdrops to life with a few simple additions. Place blue fabric on the floor to continue the Nile River into the room, and place a basket in the river. Set potted plants next to the desert. Cut red crepe paper or acetate into flame shapes and attach to the fire to give it dimension. (Optional: Add a three-dimensional decorative column to the corner of your room where the backdrops meet.)

You don't want just anybody transporting themselves through space and time! So set up the Security Checkpoint described in *Reproducible Resources* at the entrance of your room.

Bible Story Center Basics

You play a very important part in VBS, whether you are the lead teacher in the Bible Story Center or a helper. The Bible Story Center is divided into three parts to help children learn important Bible truths.

Refer to the Bible Aims for each day as you prepare each lesson. The aims help you know what learning will be taking place during your lesson. Study the Conclusion. This conversation provides an opportunity for evangelism.

Set the Story (5-10 minutes)

Choose either Option A or Option B as an introduction to the important Bible story concept. Or use them after the story for an active way to review the Bible concepts learned. If you only have 25 minutes for this center, you can omit Set the Story.

Option A

This brief group activity is designed for groups of 8 to 16 students, with one teacher for every 8 students. If you have more than 16 students, you can easily adapt the activity by duplicating it for an additional group of students—and adding another leader, of course!

Option B

This activity is similar in format to the Option A activity, but it has been written to provide an introduction to the session's Bible Memory Verse.

Tell the Story (10 minutes)

Each Bible story illustrates the Daily Mission as exemplified in the life of an Old Testament person. Display Bible story posters from *Elementary Teaching Resources* for children to see while listening to the story. Telling the story in small groups is ideal, but the story can be told effectively to a large group—just make sure additional staff members sit among children to guide children's behavior.

Introduction

Give Bibles to all students to use during the story. Consider beginning each story with a brief prayer. Then introduce the Bible story by asking a question that relates to familiar student experiences. This discussion helps children connect everyday life with the Bible lesson they are about to hear.

Bible Story

Each Bible story is written in language appropriate to the preteen age level. (Note: If you are teaching a mixed age-level group, the version found in the *Middler Bible Story Center Guide* is most appropriate for both younger and older students.) During the story, volunteers read two or three brief Scripture passages from the Bible. This shows students exactly what God's Word says. See the Storytelling Tips that precede each story for additional help.

Involvement Option

Each story includes an active listening option. These easy-to-prepare story enhancements will help keep kids actively engaged in the process.

Conclusion

After the main story, summarize the Bible truths for the children and relate the lesson to the aspect of serving God with courage that students are learning about.

New Testament Connection

Suggested near each Conclusion is a way to connect the Old Testament story to the New Testament and the life of Jesus. Use this suggested conversation to show students how God was active in people's lives throughout the Bible, just as He is active in our lives today.

Drama Option

Instead of telling the Bible story, have a team of volunteers come to each Bible Story Center and perform the Bible Story Skits from the *Assemblies and Skits Production Guide*. Or older students may enjoy performing the skits themselves.

Apply the Story (10-15 minutes)

Lead students in applying the lesson to their lives through discussion and activities in the *SFA Manuals*. This time includes:

- ◇ Bible story review
- ◇ Memory verse discussion
- ◇ Application activity and discussion
- ◇ Silent and/or group prayer

SFA Manuals

These SonForce Agency training manuals help young agents gain the skills necessary to advance from Level 1 to Level 5. Each session's *SFA Manual* page contains a Bible story review activity and a memory verse activity. To reinforce the memory verse or reward students for verse memorization, Daily Missions stickers (available from Gospel Light) can be placed on the Sticker Page, found on the inside cover of the *SFA Manual*.

Effective Teaching Tips

Preparation Is the Key

- >> Pray for God to prepare the hearts of your students.
- >> Be prepared before each day begins. Have all materials at hand, ready for use, so you can focus on the children and the learning that is taking place.
- >> Know the Daily Mission and Lesson Focus for each day and use them to connect each activity to the lesson's Bible story and memory verse.
- >> Learn and practice good storytelling techniques. (See the Storytelling Tips that accompany each story.)

Conversation Is an Art

- >> In addition to telling the Bible story, be prepared to make good use of informal conversation before and after the story. Suggestions are provided for each session to help you focus these moments toward the Bible aims.
- >> Be sensitive to each child's home situation and plan your conversation to include the variety of family situations represented in your class and among their friends. Your conversations will help you discover what a child knows (or doesn't know) about a particular topic.
- >> Review the conversation suggestions provided. Think of ways you might tailor or build on these ideas to meet the needs of the students in your class. Write down any other ideas or questions you might ask, and keep them with you during the session.
- >> Plan to listen as much as you talk. Look directly at the child who is talking. Demonstrate your interest by responding to the specific ideas the child expressed.
- >> Know each child's name and use it in positive, loving, affirming ways throughout the lesson. Look for opportunities to express praise and encouragement.
- >> Stay with your students as they complete activities. They need to know that you are there, ready to help and ready to listen.

Leading a Child to Christ

One of the greatest privileges of serving in VBS is helping children become members of God's family. Pray for the children you teach and ask God to prepare them to understand and receive the good news about Jesus. Ask God to give you the sensitivity and wisdom you need to communicate effectively and to be aware of opportunities that occur naturally.

Because children are easily influenced to follow the group, be cautious about asking for group decisions. Offer opportunities to talk and pray individually with any child who expresses interest in becoming a member of God's family—but without pressure. A good way to guard against coercing a child to respond is to simply ask, "Would you like to hear more about this now or at another time?"

When talking about salvation with children, use words and phrases they understand; never assume they understand a concept just because they can repeat certain words. Avoid symbolic terms ("born again," "ask Jesus to come into your heart," "open your heart," etc.) that will confuse these literal-minded thinkers. (You may also use the evangelism booklet *God Loves You!*)

1. God wants you to become His child. Why do you think He wants you in His family? (See 1 John 3:1.)
2. Every person in the world has done wrong things. The Bible word for doing wrong is "sin." What do you think should happen to us when we sin? (See Romans 6:23.)
3. God loves you so much that He sent His Son to die on the cross to take the punishment for your sin. Because Jesus never sinned, He is the only One who can take the punishment for your sin. (See 1 Corinthians 15:3; 1 John 4:14.)
4. Are you sorry for your sin? Tell God that you are. Do you believe Jesus died for your sin and then rose again? Tell Him that, too. If you tell God you are sorry for your sin and believe that Jesus died to take your sin away, God forgives you. (See 1 John 1:9.)
5. The Bible says that when you believe Jesus is God's Son and is alive today, you receive God's gift of eternal life. This gift makes you a child of God. (See John 3:16.) This means God is with you now and forever.

Pray for the children you teach and ask God to prepare them to understand and receive the good news about Jesus.

There is great value in encouraging a child to think and pray about what you have said before responding. Encourage the child who makes a decision to become a Christian to tell his or her parents. Give your pastor and the child's Sunday School teacher(s) his or her name. A child's initial response to Jesus is just the beginning of a lifelong process of growing in the faith, so children who make decisions need to be followed up to help them grow. The discipling booklet *Growing as God's Child* is an effective tool to use.

Moses: Boy in a Basket

Scripture

Bible Story: Exodus 1—2:10
New Testament Connection: Matthew 2:13-14

Lesson Focus

We can have courage in all situations by trusting in God's love and plans for us.

Bible Memory Verse

Blessed is the man who trusts in the Lord, whose confidence is in him. Jeremiah 17:7
Optional Enrichment Verse: *We are God's workmanship, created in Christ Jesus to do good works, which God prepared in advance for us to do.* Ephesians 2:10

SonForce Kids Special Agents
LEVEL 1
TRUST

Bible Aims

During this session, each student may
1. **DESCRIBE** the ways baby Moses' mother and sister showed courage to protect him;
2. **DISCUSS** ways in which kids can demonstrate courage by trusting in God's love and plans for them;
3. **THANK** God for His love, and ask God to help him or her have courage in specific situations;
4. **PRAY** to become a member of God's family, as the Holy Spirit leads.

Teacher Devotional

Every parent knows how stressful it can be to adjust to a new baby, but the experience of Moses' family far exceeds anything most of us will ever know. The family had a beautiful new baby boy, but Pharaoh had ordered that all Hebrew baby boys be thrown into the Nile River. Imagine trying to quiet a tiny crying baby quickly enough so that soldiers wouldn't come to kill him! As Moses grew, his parents' choices were few; if he were discovered, he would die. They did have an idea, however: They put him in the Nile in a waterproof basket. They did all they could, TRUSTING God to do something miraculous.

God had big plans for Moses. He protected Moses and used him mightily. Now think about your own life. You've seen God protect you, perhaps even through some times as dangerous as those Moses faced. Pause to consider what His plans may be for you! Those plans may not look big to you—they may even be hidden from your sight right now—but rest assured, they are of eternal importance!

There are no little plans in God's eyes. What you are doing at this moment is part of the amazing tapestry He is weaving for you and through you. In His plan, your words and actions will affect many others. He has led you and protected you just as He protected Moses. Trust in God as you watch His plans unfold!

1\. Set the Story (5-10 minutes)

Option A: Guess the Question

Preparation

If you only have 25 minutes for this center, omit Set the Story. Photocopy and cut apart Agent Identification Cards, making at least two cards for each student. Hide cards in classroom.

Materials Checklist

- ◇ *SonForce Kids CD* and player
- ◇ Agent Identification Cards (p. 40)
- ◇ scissors or paper cutter

Procedure

Play "God's Kids" from CD as students search for cards. Students search to find two different cards. If a student finds a card he or she already has, the card is placed back where it was found. When each student has found two different cards, he or she sits down in the center of the room, keeping cards hidden from other students.

When all students have been seated, ask students holding cards with the number one to come forward. Students say their names aloud and then silently read the question written on the card. Ask each student in turn to answer the question aloud—but not to say the question itself. Other students guess what the question is. Continue for all eight cards or as time permits.

Conversation

One way special agents know how to recognize each other is by learning facts about each other. Getting to know others better helps us to build trust with each other.

>> **What does it mean to trust someone?** (Believe that he or she will be honest with you. Believe that he or she will do what's good for you.)

>> **What are some things you might notice about a person that show that you can trust him or her?** (That he or she is honest. That he or she treats other people well.)

>> **How can we show that we trust someone?** (Believe what the person says. Ask the person for help.)

Today we're going to find out what it means to be special agents for God and to trust Him every day.

Option B: Back It Up

Preparation

Photocopy and cut out verse cards, making one for each student. Practice saying the names of two or three students backward. For example, "Megan" becomes "nagem" and "Sam" becomes "mas."

Materials Checklist

- ◇ Bibles
- ◇ Back It Up Cards (p. 41)
- ◇ scissors
- ◇ pencils

Hello, Nagem! How are you Mas?

Procedure

Introduce the activity by calling two or three students by their name backward. Once students figure out what you are doing, help all of them to say their names backward.

Hand a verse card to each student. **Special agents sometimes need to solve codes. See if you can crack this one!** Allow several minutes for students to figure out the code on their own. For students still having trouble deciphering the code, give a hint or two. **Remember what we did with our names. How could that help you solve the code?** If after several minutes students are still having trouble, give the solution or ask a student who discovered the solution to tell the solution. **Each word of the message is spelled backward!** If time and interest allow, have students write the message correctly at the bottom of the page.

Enrichment Option

Photocopy "Top Secret Code" from page 39. Tape or glue to a large manila envelope. Before class, place verse cards in envelope. Then, introduce activity by saying **Let's look in our Special Agent Code envelope and see what today's code is!** Do this each day to introduce the activity.

Conversation

These words tell us an important message that God gave us in the Bible.

>> **Who does this verse tell us is blessed?** Volunteers respond. **This verse uses the word "man," but it means anyone—women and children, too!**

>> **How do we know we can trust or have confidence in God?** (God loves us. God always tells the truth. God never fails us. God is always with us and helps us.)

>> **How can trusting in God help us have courage?** (When we trust God, we know He'll always take care of us. Knowing that God will always be with us and help us makes us feel strong.)

Trusting in God can help us every day. Today we're going to find out how.

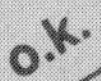

2. Tell the Story (10 minutes)

Moses: Boy in a Basket

Exodus 1—2:10

Preparation

Display Session 1 Bible Story Poster. Use Post-it Notes to mark Exodus 1 in students' Bibles. Distribute Bibles to students.

Materials Checklist

- ◇ Session 1 Bible Story Poster from *Elementary Teaching Resources*
- ◇ Post-it Notes

For each student and teacher—

- ◇ Bible

Storytelling Tip

Teach from the Bible, not your curriculum. Students need to see you as a teacher of God's Word—not merely a reader of a curriculum product. Have your Bible open in front of you throughout the story and clearly state that the story is true: "This story happened to real people. We know the story is true because it comes from God's Word, the Bible."

Involvement Option

Before the story, each student draws a stick figure to represent Miriam. Lead students to add five or six blank lines with arrows to represent things Miriam was thinking, feeling, doing, hearing, seeing, saying, etc. (See sketch.) As you tell story, students fill in blank lines with appropriate responses. A helper may complete a similar stick figure on a large sheet of butcher paper.

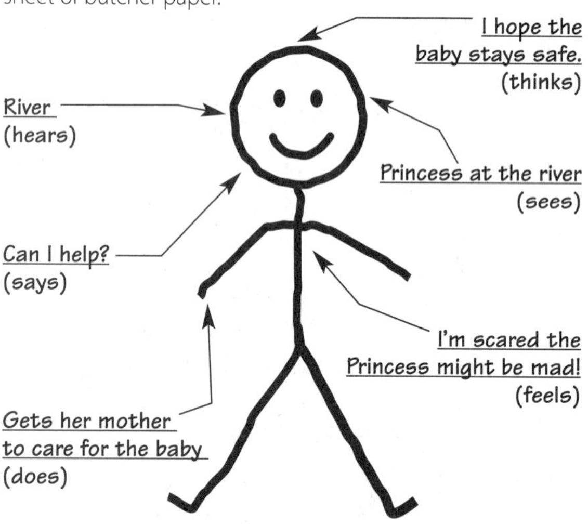

Introduction

Where would you hide something VERY important? Volunteers respond. **Today we're going to hear about a mother and daughter who showed courage and hid something very important. The story comes from the book of Exodus in your Bibles.** (Optional: Invite students familiar with this story to tell story details. Supplement as needed, referring students to Bible Story Poster for help.)

A Pharaoh's Fear

A long time ago, the land of Egypt was ruled by powerful kings called pharaohs. People from many lands lived in Egypt. But for one group of people, the Israelites, life was about to become very hard. A new pharaoh became ruler, and he didn't like the Israelites one little bit! "There are too many Israelites living here," Pharaoh told his leaders. "What if they join our enemies and fight against us?"

"You're right," the men agreed. "The Israelites are dangerous."

"Those Israelites will become my slaves," the Pharaoh decided. "They'll work from morning to night making bricks."

Pharaoh's orders were carried out immediately—and harshly! The Egyptian taskmasters used whips to make them work harder. The Israelite slaves built two large cities. And many of them were forced to do back-breaking work in the fields, too.

An odd thing happened, though. As the years went by, Pharaoh noticed that there seemed to be more and more Israelites. He was hoping to DECREASE the number of Israelites, but instead their numbers INCREASED.

Well, this made the Egyptians even more afraid, so they made the Israelites work even harder!

But Pharaoh didn't stop there. He gave his people some terrible orders. "Drown all the Israelite baby boys," he said. "Throw them into the Nile River." With this plan,

Pharaoh made SURE there would be fewer, and not more, Israelite men who might rebel and fight.

One Israelite family was determined they would NOT let Pharaoh kill their baby boy. The mother hid her baby son and was very careful to make sure no one knew about the baby. For three months the family kept their baby a secret. **What would you do to keep a baby a secret? What problems might you have?**

A Parent's Plan

The baby's mother had an idea of how to keep the baby safe. **Read Exodus 2:3 to find out what she did.** She made a basket out of reeds and covered it with tar and pitch to make it waterproof. Then she put her baby boy in the basket and hid it among the reeds along the bank of the Nile River. The baby's older sister, Miriam, was given the job of watching the basket to see what would happen. The mother told Miriam, "Watch him carefully." The mother loved this baby so much! She didn't want him to get hurt.

"Yes, mother," Miriam said. She loved her little brother, too.

Miriam hid in the tall reeds beside the river and watched as the basket floated on the water. Then she heard voices. Some women were coming down to the river to bathe. Miriam peeked through the reeds. She held her breath—afraid to move. Miriam could hardly believe her eyes! It was the princess—Pharaoh's own daughter—and her servants! Would they see the basket?

"That looks like a basket over there," the princess said. "Go see what is in it," she told her maid. They HAD seen the basket!

A Royal Rescue

The maid went into the water and brought back the basket. "Look! There's a baby inside!" she said.

The baby cried and the princess felt sorry for him. "This is one of the Israelite babies," she said as she held him close. "Look how beautiful he is!"

Meanwhile, Miriam was still watching from her place among the reeds. **What would you have done if you were Miriam?** When Miriam saw that the princess felt sorry for the baby, Miriam stepped out into the open and asked, "Would you like me to find one of the Israelite women to nurse the baby for you?"

"Yes," answered the princess, "go and do that."

So Miriam ran to find someone who could take care of the baby. Of course, she immediately went to her own mother and brought her back to the princess!

Read what the princess told Miriam's mother in Exodus 2:9. Now the baby was safe! No one would try to hurt a baby that belonged to the princess—and the baby got to live with his family for a while! The princess named the baby "Moses," which in Egyptian means "is born." The name "Moses" also sounds like the Hebrew word meaning "to draw out." His name would remind the princess, and anyone else who knew this story, that Moses was drawn out of the river.

When Moses grew to be a young boy, he went to live in the palace with the princess. Even though Moses grew up in the Egyptian Pharaoh's palace, he knew that he was really an Israelite. And Moses didn't like the way the Pharaoh treated the Israelites. When Moses grew up, God chose him to lead the Israelites out of Egypt to a new land that God would give to them.

Conclusion

Moses' mother and sister must have been terrified for him—and for themselves! Moses and his family were in real danger. But God had a plan for Moses—and because of his family's courage, Moses grew up to do a very important mission for God. No matter how small or how big our worries or fears are, we know that God has a plan for us. Even if we don't always understand God's plans, we can always trust that He loves us and His plans are good! Trusting in God's plans helps us to have courage in ALL situations.

New Testament Connection

In Matthew 2:13-14 in the New Testament, the Bible tells of a time when Mary and Joseph had to have courage, too. An angel appeared to Joseph in a dream and told him that King Herod wanted to kill baby Jesus. God's plan was for Mary and Joseph to take Jesus to Egypt and live there until it was safe to return home. Mary and Joseph trusted in God's plan to keep Jesus safe. They knew that God's plans are always the best! They followed God's plan in spite of Herod's threats.

Focus on Evangelism

God loves us. He has many good plans for each one of us. However, His greatest plan of all was to create a way for us to become members of His family. Invite students interested in knowing more about becoming members of God's family to talk with you or another teacher after class. (See "Leading a Child to Christ," p. 8.)

3. Apply the Story
(10-15 minutes)

Bible Story Review

To review Bible story, students complete "Character Profile" activity on Level 1 page. **Why did Pharaoh want to kill the Israelite boys?** (He thought there were too many Israelites. He was afraid that if the Israelites had enough strong men they would attack him.) **At the river, what else could Miriam have chosen to do?** (She could have run away. She could have stayed hidden.) **How did the actions of Miriam and her mother show courage? Why do you think Miriam had the courage to talk to the princess?**

Just as God had a plan to save Moses, He has a plan for each one of us, too! God has plans for us because He loves us. Indicate the Daily Mission logo on the page. **Each day at SonForce Kids, we'll be given a new Daily Mission. Each Daily Mission tells SonForce agents something the Bible teaches about courage. Today's Daily Mission is to "TRUST in God's Plans." God has made each one of us able to contribute something good to the world around us. By trusting in God's love and plans for us we can have courage in all situations.**

Materials Checklist

◇ *SFA Manual* Level 1 pages
◇ colored markers
◇ slips of paper
◇ small basket

Optional—

◇ *SFA Manual* Sticker Pages
◇ Daily Missions stickers

Enrichment Option

If, instead of doing a paper activity, you want to get kids up on their feet, use the Bible Story Review Game written specifically for each Bible story and available in the *Bible Games Center Guide.* Make sure to coordinate your game plans with the leader of the Bible Games Center.

Memory Verse/Application

Students turn Level 1 page over. Ask a volunteer to read memory verse aloud. **What does this verse tell us to do when we need courage?** (Trust God. Put our confidence in Him.) **Courage doesn't mean not having any fear. Courage means being willing to act, even when we are afraid or worried.**

When are some times a kid your age might need courage? (When giving a presentation at school. When parents have an argument.) For each situation named, ask, **How could it help a kid in that situation to trust in God's love and plans? How could a kid in that situation demonstrate courage?** Students complete "Level 1 Mission" activity. (Optional: Give each student a Daily Missions sticker for verse memorization to place on the Sticker Page.)

Prayer

What are some situations kids might face in which they would need courage? Write each situation named on a separate slip of paper, and then fold slips and place them inside a small basket. Ask volunteers to each take a paper slip and hold on to it. Lead class in prayer, thanking God for His love. Allow time for volunteers to ask God to help them have courage in the situations listed on the strips of paper they drew from the basket. Close prayer by thanking God for giving us courage in all situations.

Esther: Queen at Risk

Scripture

Bible Story: Esther 2—8
New Testament Connection: Matthew 4:18-22; Mark 3:13-19

Lesson Focus

We can have courage to stand up for others by uniting with God's people.

Bible Memory Verse

Be devoted to one another in brotherly love. Honor one another above yourselves. Romans 12:10
Optional Enrichment Verse: *Each of you should look not only to your own interests, but also to the interests of others.* Philippians 2:4

Bible Aims

During this session, each student may
1. **DESCRIBE** how Esther, by uniting with God's people, had the courage to stand up for them;
2. **DETERMINE** words and actions that are ways of standing up for others;
3. **ASK** God to help him or her have courage to stand up for others;
4. **PRAY** to become a member of God's family, as the Holy Spirit leads.

Teacher Devotional

During the rule of Xerxes (also known by the Hebrew name Ahasuerus) of Persia occurs the beautiful and charming story of Esther. Although God's name is not mentioned in the book of Esther, His presence can be found behind each word. God has a part in all the events of human life.

Esther stands out as God's chosen one. The beauty of Esther was that she wasn't spoiled by her great position. Though she became queen of a great king, she didn't forget the kindness of her cousin Mordecai, who had brought her up from childhood. Esther was faced with the opportunity to help rescue the lives of her oppressed people, the Jews, but only at great risk to her own life. Accepting this dangerous task, she carried it out with courage and wisdom. Even as she went forward on behalf of the Jews, she asked them to pray and fast on HER behalf. Esther knew that God was listening to the prayers of His people and that with His help they could UNITE and defeat their enemy.

It was a daring act for her to enter unsummoned into the presence of the king. Yet she knew she must choose the right course, despite the danger to herself. She knew this was a time to have courage and stand up for others. Esther was prepared and was brought to the kingdom for just such an hour.

We would all do well to pause and ask, "Why has God allowed me to live at this particular hour?" When faced with challenges that require the courage to do what is right, it is always easier when we are supported by the prayers of fellow believers.

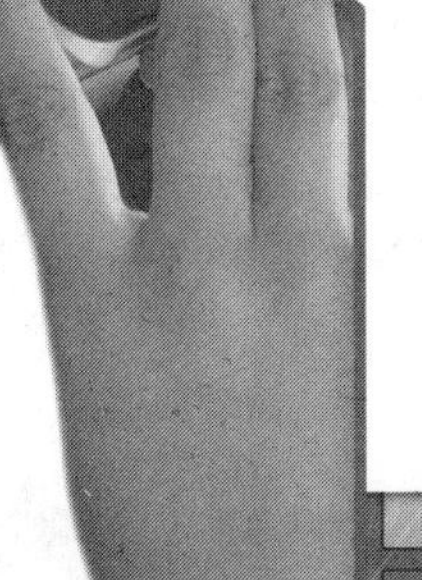

1. Set the Story (5-10 minutes)

Option A: Rocket Races

Preparation

If you only have 25 minutes for this center, omit Set the Story. Photocopy and cut out a set of People Cards for each team. Place each team's cards in a separate pile at one end of the playing area. Make a masking-tape line about 10 to 20 feet (3 to 6 m) from the sets of cards. On each sheet of construction paper, draw a rocket ship or photocopy a rocket-ship pattern from *Reproducible Resources*.

Materials Checklist

- ◇ People Cards (p. 42)
- ◇ scissors or paper cutter
- ◇ masking tape

For each team of 4 or 6 students—

- ◇ 2 sheets of construction paper

Procedure

Students divide into teams of four or six. Students then pair up to form partners within their team. Each team lines up behind masking-tape line, opposite a set of cards. Hand the first pair in each line two sheets of construction paper with rocket ships. One partner in each pair with papers places one paper on the floor. The other partner stands facing the team and steps backward onto the paper. Then the partner with the papers places the second paper closer to pile of cards and the other partner steps backward onto it.

Students continue placing papers and stepping back onto them to make their way across the playing area. When a pair reaches their team's pile of cards, each partner takes a card. The pair then returns to their team, switching roles so that the partner who had been placing papers now steps on them. Then they give papers to the next players on their team, and the game continues in relay fashion until all cards have been collected. First team to finish selects a card and tells about the person whose picture is on the card. Continue, rotating among teams until all cards have been discussed.

Conversation

Your job as Level 2 agents is to identify people who need your help.

>> **Which of these cards reminds you of someone you know?**

>> **How might (your grandpa) need help?**

>> **What does it mean to stand up for the needs of others?** (To notice ways to help them. To be concerned about their needs. To try to help them.)

Today we're going to talk about a woman who needed a lot of courage to stand up for the needs of others.

Option B: Zig and Zag

Preparation

Photocopy and cut out verse cards, making one for each student.

Materials Checklist

- ◇ Bibles
- ◇ Zigzag Verse Cards (p. 43)
- ◇ scissors
- ◇ pencils

Procedure

Hand a verse card to each student. **We've got a new code for all you special agents to crack! How can you connect the letters to make words?** Allow several minutes for students to figure out the code on their own. For students still having trouble deciphering the code, give a hint or two. **It looks like the lines are grouped together—two lines to a group. How could you use both lines together?** If after several minutes students are still having trouble, give the solution or ask a student who discovered the solution to tell the solution. **Starting with the top of the two lines, zigzag up and down from one letter to the next: B, e, d, e and so on. Write the letters in order at the bottom of the page.**

Conversation

- **According to our verse, what are we supposed to show one another?** (Devotion. Brotherly love. Honor.)
- **What do you think "brotherly love" means?** (Caring for others as we would for someone in our own family.)
- **What are some ways to show brotherly love to others?** (Don't make fun of others. Help someone with a chore. Let someone else choose which video game to play. Stand up for them.)

Joining with others—or "uniting" with them—can give us courage to help others. Today we're going to talk about ways to help each other do what Romans 12:10 says to do.

Enrichment Option

Provide scrap paper so that kids can use this zigzag code to write messages of their own.

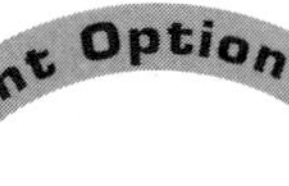

Tell the Story 2.
(10 minutes)

Esther: Queen at Risk

Esther 2—8

Preparation

Display Session 2 Bible Story Poster. Use Post-it Notes to mark Esther 2 in students' Bibles.

Materials Checklist

- ◇ Session 2 Bible Story Poster from *Elementary Teaching Resources*
- ◇ Post-it Notes

For each student and teacher—

- ◇ Bible

Storytelling Tip

For a fun alternative or supplement to this or any Bible story, ask teachers, helpers or student volunteers to perform the Bible story skits found in the *Assemblies and Skits Production Guide.*

Involvement Option

Every year Jewish people celebrate Purim to remember Esther's story. Purim includes audience participation similar to a melodrama. On separate sheets of construction paper, print "Hooray!" and "Boo!" Before telling story, hold up signs and practice responding by saying the words with emotion. At appropriate times during the story, hold up signs and lead students' response. (For example, hold up "Hooray" after saying, ". . . he chose Esther to be the next queen!" and "Boo!" after saying, ". . . he planned to DESTROY not just Mordecai but ALL the Jewish people!")

Introduction

Have you ever had to talk to someone who you thought might be mad at you? How did you feel before you talked to the person? Today we're going to hear about a woman who was probably afraid to talk to someone—the king of Persia! (Optional: Invite students familiar with this story to tell story details. Supplement as needed, referring students to Bible Story Poster for help.)

A Beautiful Bride

Many years ago in Persia, there lived a girl named Esther. Her family was one of many Jewish families who had been taken as captives from their homes in Israel many years before. When Esther's parents died, she lived with her cousin Mordecai (MOR-dih-ki). He cared for Esther as she grew into a beautiful young woman.

One day, the king of Persia announced that he was looking for a new queen. Esther was one of many young women chosen to come to the palace and prepare to meet him. For a whole year, the women were given special beauty treatments. They put expensive oils and perfumes on their skin to make it soft and sweet-smelling. The women were given beautiful clothes to wear, and their hair was brushed until it was shiny and smooth.

The day came for the king to meet the women. They put on their best clothes and made themselves as beautiful as they could. One by one, the king met each of the young women. Of all the women, Esther was his favorite, and he chose her to be his queen.

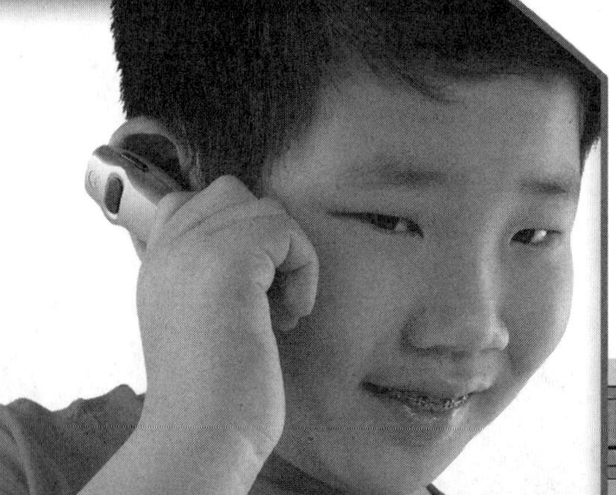

A Perilous Plot

About this time, the king promoted a man named Haman to be in charge of the other government officials. Haman was so proud of his new job, he started demanding that everyone bow down to him! But Esther's cousin Mordecai, who also worked for the king, refused to bow down. Mordecai didn't mean to be disrespectful. But as a Jew, he believed that he should only bow to God. Mordecai's refusal made Haman so angry that he planned a way to destroy not just Mordecai, but ALL the Jewish people!

Read Esther 3:8-9 to find out what Haman said to the king. Haman made the Jewish people sound so dangerous that the king gave Haman permission to KILL them!

Orders to kill the Jewish people were soon sent throughout the land. Mordecai heard the terrible news and knew he had to act! He sent a message to Queen Esther, telling her about Haman's plan and asking her to beg the king for help.

At first Esther was reluctant to do what Mordecai wanted. **Read Esther 4:10-11 to find out why.** Historians say that some Persian kings sat on their thrones surrounded by men with axes ready to punish anyone who came to the king without being summoned. The only way the person could be saved was if the king gave that person a pardon by holding out his scepter.

Mordecai reminded Esther that it was no accident she had been chosen queen. Perhaps she had become queen just for this opportunity to save the Jewish people! Even though she was queen, that wouldn't save her life if EVERY Jewish person was to be killed.

Esther asked Mordecai to have the Jewish people in the city fast—go without food—for three days. This was to help them focus on prayer and show God they were serious about needing His help! Esther also fasted for three days. She promised to go to the king no matter what the outcome might be.

After Esther's three-day fast, she put on her royal robes and her best perfumes. Then she stood in the inner court of the palace. To her relief, the king held out his scepter. He asked, "What is your request, my queen? I'll give you anything you want."

"All I ask is that you come to a banquet I have prepared for you and Haman."

A Bountiful Banquet

The king must have wondered what was so important that Esther was willing to risk her life! At the banquet the king asked again what she wanted, but Queen Esther only asked him to come back for another banquet the next day.

Haman felt very important because HE was the only one who had the honor of being invited to the queen's banquet with the king. On the way home from the banquet, Haman felt great! THEN he saw Mordecai. Mordecai didn't bow down. Haman was FURIOUS! Haman ordered that gallows be built so that Mordecai could be hanged!

That night, the king couldn't sleep. So he read the royal records and discovered that Mordecai had saved his life by reporting an assassination plot. The records indicated that nothing had been done to thank Mordecai for saving the king. So the king ordered Haman to honor Mordecai. **How do you think Haman felt about that?**

During the second banquet, the king offered to give Esther whatever she wanted—up to half of his entire kingdom! Queen Esther answered, "If you're pleased with me, please rescue me and my people. We've been sentenced to death!"

The king was shocked. He demanded to know who was threatening the life of his queen! "It's that man—that vile Haman!" Esther answered.

The king was enraged! He ordered Haman to be hanged. He also gave everything that Haman owned to Esther. The king gave Esther and Mordecai permission to write a new law so that the Jews could defend themselves against attack.

Conclusion

Esther's courageous actions made a HUGE difference to her people. But you don't have to be a king or queen to make a difference! God can use anyone who is willing to serve Him. When we stand up for others, we make a difference to them. But we don't have to do it alone! Uniting with others who follow God can help us have the courage we need to stand up for others.

New Testament Connection

In Matthew 4:18-22 and Mark 3:13-19, we read about Jesus calling 12 men to be His disciples—special agents for God! These men made a difference in the lives of other people by working together to serve God. They followed Jesus and helped Him throughout His ministry here on Earth, and continued following Jesus even after He returned to heaven.

Focus on Evangelism

When we become members of God's family, we unite with others to love and obey God. Invite students interested in knowing more about becoming members of God's family to talk with you or another teacher after class. (See "Leading a Child to Christ," p. 8.)

3. Apply the Story
(10-15 minutes)

Bible Story Review

To review Bible story, students complete "Character Profile" activity on Level 2 page. **Why did Haman want Mordecai to be killed?** (Mordecai didn't bow down to him.) **Why was Esther afraid to approach the king?** (Because the king hadn't invited her, she knew that he might choose to have her killed.) **Why do you think Esther had the courage to stand up for her people despite the danger?**

Esther asked Mordecai and the other Jewish people to unite with her by fasting and praying to God. Their love and support helped her get the courage she needed to stand up for them. Indicate the Daily Mission logo on the page. **Today's Daily Mission is to "UNITE with God's People." Just like Esther, uniting with God's people can give us the courage to stand up for others.**

Materials Checklist

- ◇ *SFA Manual* Level 2 pages
- ◇ colored markers
- ◇ small Post-it Notes
- ◇ ruler

Optional—

- ◇ *SFA Manual* Sticker Pages
- ◇ Daily Missions stickers

Memory Verse/Application

Students turn Level 2 page over. Ask a volunteer to read memory verse aloud. **What does it mean to honor others more than yourself?** (To treat them with respect. To put their needs ahead of your own.) **One way to honor others is to stand up for them. What are some situations in which kids your age can stand up for others?** (When they are being picked on or falsely accused. When people are spreading gossip about them. When others are ignoring their needs.) **How could uniting with a friend help us to stand up for others?** (It could give us courage. The friend might have ideas of what could be done. It's easier to do something with a friend.) Students complete "Level 2 Mission" activity. (Optional: Give each student a Daily Missions sticker for verse memorization to place on the Sticker Page.)

Teaching Tip

Be sure each student in your group hears at least one specific compliment from you sometime during the session. Your comments will help students focus on doing what's right.

Prayer

Hold up ruler. **I don't have a king's scepter, so this ruler will have to do! When are some specific times we can ask God to give us courage to stand up for others?** Write each response on a separate small Post-it Note and stick each note to ruler, overlapping if necessary. Lead class in prayer, asking for God's courage to stand up for others. Pass ruler around the class, allowing volunteers to pull off one Post-it Note and ask for God's help to have courage in the situation named on the note. Close prayer by thanking God for helping us have courage to stand up for others.

Daniel: Servant of God

Scripture

Bible Story: Daniel 1
New Testament Connection: Matthew 5—7

Lesson Focus

We can have courage to make wise choices by training to serve God.

Bible Memory Verse

Listen to advice and accept instruction, and in the end you will be wise. Proverbs 19:20

Optional Enrichment Verse: *The Lord gives wisdom, and from his mouth come knowledge and understanding.* Proverbs 2:6

Bible Aims

During this session, each student may

1. **SUMMARIZE** the wise and courageous choices Daniel made because he had trained to serve God;
2. **DESCRIBE** ways that kids can train for God's service and the benefits that result;
3. **ASK** God to help him or her have courage to make wise choices, and plan a way to train for God's service;
4. **PRAY** to become a member of God's family, as the Holy Spirit leads.

Teacher Devotional

Imagine living through an enemy attack that destroys your home and makes you a prisoner of war. Daniel and his friends lived through just this horror, probably while they were still teenagers. The best and brightest of Jerusalem's royal court, they saw their promising futures and privileged circumstances evaporate as they left Jerusalem behind.

Captive in a strange land, they were without a country or a chosen future. The Babylonians were clearly working to eliminate their Israelite identities and make them ready to serve Nebuchadnezzar. The boys probably had no choice about being dressed in Babylonian fashion or given Babylonian names. But there was one way they could hold on to who they really were: They could honor the dietary laws of Israel. It may seem like a small thing to us, but it was one way to be obedient and remain true to the training they had received to serve God.

God often brings such small acts to our attention, acts we can do to continue to put into practice our love and obedience to God. These small acts may not seem any more significant than the food choices of Daniel and his friends. It's usually easier to ignore such small things and go along with "the program." But remembering the ways in which we have been trained will help us obey God with the courage of Daniel. When we're tempted to go along with the crowd, God gives us courage and strength to stand up for His ways like Daniel and his friends did.

Set the Story 1. (5-10 minutes)

Option A: Agents in Training

Preparation

If you only have 25 minutes for this center, omit Set the Story. On slips of paper, write objects that might be used in special-agent training (cell phone, camera, badge, computer, car, etc.). Include some random objects as well (ice skates, screwdriver, trumpet, toothbrush, etc.). Place paper slips inside bag. Attach a large sheet of paper to the wall at a height that students can easily reach.

Materials Checklist

- ◇ slips of paper
- ◇ pen
- ◇ paper lunch bag
- ◇ large sheets of paper
- ◇ wide-tip marker

Procedure

Play a game like Pictionary. A volunteer draws a slip of paper from the bag and silently reads the object on the paper. He or she uses marker to draw one or more pictures until someone guesses the object. Once the object is identified, other students tell a way a special agent might use the object. The student who guessed the object becomes the drawer for the next round or chooses another volunteer to draw.

Conversation

Special agents use many different types of objects in their training to perform their duties. As followers of God, we're like special agents for God. We can learn to make wise choices as we train to love and obey God.

>> **As a special agent for God, what is something that might help you in your training?** (Bible. Prayer. People who know and love God.)

>> **As a special agent for God, how can you learn more about making wise choices?** (Read the Bible. Go to church and Sunday School. Talk with others about God.)

>> **Who are some people who could help you with your training to be a special agent for God?** (Parents. Pastors. Sunday School teacher. VBS leaders and helpers.)

Today we're going to hear a true story about a man named Daniel. We'll talk about some of the choices Daniel made after he trained to serve God.

Teaching Tip

If a student tells a violent way to use one of the objects, suggest that instead, he or she share a way to use the object for good.

Option B: Tic-Tac-Toe Training

Preparation

Photocopy and cut out the Answer Key and Tic-Tac-Toe Cards, making one of each for every student.

Materials Checklist

- ◇ Bibles
- ◇ Tic-Tac-Toe Cards (p. 44)
- ◇ scissors
- ◇ scrap paper
- ◇ pencils

Procedure

Pass out scrap paper and pencils. Hand a Tic-Tac-Toe Card to each student. **Today's code uses symbols instead of letters.** Allow several minutes for students to figure out the code on their own, using the Tic-Tac-Toe Code on each card. Students write verse on pieces of scrap paper. If after several minutes students are still having difficulty deciphering the code, hand out copies of the Answer Key. Provide individual help as needed until each student has completed the code.

Conversation

>> **According to our verse, how does a person become wise?** (By listening to advice and accepting instruction from others who know and love God.)

>> **Who are some people who could give us good advice and instruction?** (Parents. Pastors. Sunday School teachers. VBS teachers and helpers.)

>> **When are some times it would be good to be wise and know what to do?** (When a situation is scary. When we're someplace new. When someone is being mean.)

Making wise choices doesn't always come naturally to us. It's something we train to do. Today we're going to talk about how we can train for God's service and do what Proverbs 19:20 says.

Tell the Story (10 minutes) **2.**

Daniel: Servant of God

Daniel 1

Preparation

Display the Session 3 Bible Story Poster. Use Post-it Notes to mark Daniel 1 in students' Bibles. Distribute Bibles to students.

Materials Checklist

- ◇ Session 3 Bible Story Poster from *Elementary Teaching Resources*
- ◇ Post-it Notes

For each student and teacher—

- ◇ Bible

Storytelling Tip

Ask the questions provided in the Introduction of each story. These questions will help students know what to focus on as the stories are told. Use the suggested questions and Scripture lookups included in the story. If you don't have enough Bibles for all your students, have at least one they can share. These questions guide student discovery of Bible-story facts. Students will remember what they discover for themselves longer than the things they merely hear a leader tell them.

Involvement Option

Before class begins, cut a variety of vegetables into pieces. Students eat vegetables as you tell the story. (Optional: Provide small cups with dip for students to dip vegetables into.)

Introduction

If you could choose a new name for yourself, what would it be? Volunteers respond. **How would you feel if someone made you change your name to something you didn't like? In today's story we're going to learn about some people who were given new names that they didn't really want.** (Optional: Invite students familiar with this story to tell story details. Supplement as needed, referring students to Bible Story Poster for help.)

Trained to Serve God

The book of Daniel in the Bible tells us about a time when the country of Judah was under attack. Nebuchadnezzar (neh-buh-kuhd-NEH-zuhr), the king of Babylon, had sent his armies to invade Jerusalem! Enemy soldiers took thousands of captives away, forcing them away from their homes and taking them to Babylon. Among the captives were four young men named Daniel, Hananiah (han-uh-NI-uh), Mishael (MEE-shah-el) and Azariah (az-uh-RI-uh).

Usually when a king conquered another country, the men in the land would be put to death or treated as slaves and forced to do backbreaking work. But Nebuchadnezzar gave an unexpected order. **Read Daniel 1:3-4 to find out what Nebuchadnezzar wanted his chief official to do.**

Nebuchadnezzar planned for these young men to be treated very well. Their days would be spent in learning. They were even to be given the same food the king ate! And at the end of three years of training, they would work as advisors to the king.

So when Daniel and his three friends found out they were chosen for this special training, they may have considered themselves to be very lucky—even though they had been forced to leave their families and their country.

Trained to Honor God

Nebuchadnezzar's chief official was given the job of supervising the training and care of these young men. The first thing he did was to change their Hebrew names to Babylonian names. The four young men became known as Belteshazzar (belt-uh-SHAH-zuhr), Shadrach (SHAHD-rahk), Meshach (MEE-shahk) and Abednego (uh-BEHD-nee-goh). **Why do you think the official did this? How do you think Daniel and his friends felt about their new names?**

Though the Bible doesn't give a reason for changing their names, the chief official may have wanted Daniel and his friends to think of themselves as Babylonians now instead of Jews. For example, Daniel's name, which means "God is my Judge," was changed to Belteshazzar, which means "Marduk, protect my life!" In fact, ALL of their new names referred to the false gods worshiped by the Babylonians.

Even though Nebuchadnezzar hadn't ordered these young men to worship the false Babylonian gods, Daniel still had a big problem. The problem was with the food he and his friends were supposed to eat.

Trained to Obey God

Before he entered into the king's training, Daniel had been trained according to the laws that God had given to Moses. And those laws said that the Israelites were not to eat certain kinds of meat or meat that hadn't been prepared in a certain way. There was another problem, too: The king's food had probably been used for worshiping the false gods of the Babylonian people. Eating that food would be like worshiping the false gods—and if they did that, they would be dishonoring God!

Daniel went to see the chief official. "Please don't force me to eat this food that will offend God," Daniel pleaded. **Why was Daniel's decision risky?** The chief official could have become angry with Daniel for insulting the king's food. Daniel could have been thrown into prison, or worse. **Read Daniel 1:9 to find out how God helped Daniel in this situation.**

"Look, I feel sorry for you," the chief official replied, "but the king would be awfully angry with me if I disobeyed his orders. And don't think he wouldn't notice. He'd take one look at how thin and weak you'd get from not eating, and he would have my head!"

But Daniel didn't give up. He talked to the guard who brought them their food. **Read Daniel 1:12-13 to find out what Daniel said.** The guard must have been very surprised at Daniel's request. After all, eating the king's food, and looking very well-fed as a result, was a sign of honor and prestige. But he agreed to the test.

The guard may have been very nervous when he checked on Daniel and his friends after 10 days. *Will they be OK?* he might have wondered. *If they aren't, can I get them healthy again before the king sees them?* But to his surprise, Daniel and his friends actually looked BETTER than the other young men! So the guard allowed them to make their food choice permanent.

At the end of the three years of training, the chief official took all the young men to the king. The king looked at them and talked with each one; but his favorites were Daniel, Shadrach, Meshach and Abednego. God gave these four young men more wisdom than the king's own advisors.

Conclusion

Daniel and his friends had just been chosen to train to serve the Babylonian king. But they had been training to serve God all of their lives! Because they had studied God's Word and knew His rules, they were able to make the wisest choice. Knowing that their actions would please God gave them the courage they needed to continue serving Him.

Like Daniel, each of us will face times when it's hard to know the right thing to do. But when we TRAIN to serve God, He will help us to make the wisest choice—and he'll give us the courage to do it!

New Testament Connection

In the New Testament, we read about how Jesus trained His disciples to serve Him. Every day, as the disciples traveled with Jesus, they listened as He talked about God and how to please Him. Matthew 5—7 tells about Jesus' Sermon on the Mount, in which He gave His disciples training on how to serve God with their attitudes as well as their actions.

Focus on Evangelism

Before someone can train to serve God, he or she must first become a member of His family. Talk with interested students about becoming members of God's family (see "Leading a Child to Christ" on p. 8).

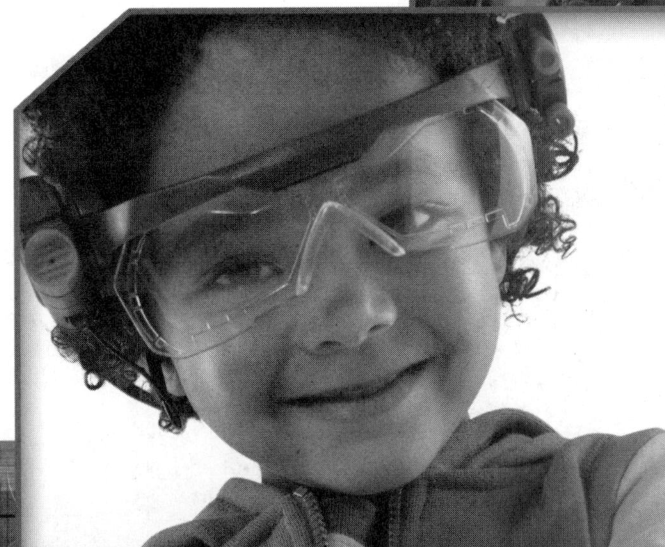

3. Apply the Story (10-15 minutes)

Bible Story Review

To review Bible story, students complete "Character Profile" activity on Level 3 page. **Why didn't Daniel want to eat meat from the king's table?** (He had been taught only to eat meat which had been prepared in a certain way. He had been taught never to eat food which had been used for worshiping false gods.) **What risks was Daniel taking by choosing not to eat the meat?** (The king might have become angry. Daniel and his friends might have become tired and weak.) **What else could Daniel have said to the chief official?** ("We'll eat the meat." "You can't make us eat that meat!")

Indicate the Daily Mission logo on the page. **Today's Daily Mission is to "TRAIN for God's Service." Daniel and his friends were in training to serve the Babylonian king; but they had spent their whole lives training to serve God. Because of their training, they knew what God wanted them to do and they had the courage they needed to make wise choices. In the same way, when WE train to serve God we'll be given courage we need to make wise choices.**

Materials Checklist

- ◇ *SFA Manual* Level 3 pages
- ◇ colored markers
- ◇ sheet of paper
- ◇ clipboard

Optional—

- ◇ *SFA Manual* Sticker Pages
- ◇ Daily Missions stickers

Enrichment Option

Provide several shapes cut from craft foam. On shapes, students write one or more things they intend to do to train as special agents serving God. Kids glue magnets to backs of shapes and take home as reminders.

Memory Verse/Application

Students turn Level 3 page over. Ask a volunteer to read memory verse aloud. **What do you think it means to be wise?** (To make good choices.) **People aren't born knowing how to make wise choices. What are some ways we can learn how to make wise choices?** (Obey God's Word. By learning from our mistakes. By listening to other people.) **How would knowing how to make wise choices help us in everyday life?** (It would help us to avoid actions that could hurt ourselves or others. It could give us the courage to do what's right.)

The activity on this page will help you think about ways that we can train for God's service. Students complete "Level 3 Mission" activity. (Optional: Give each student a Daily Missions sticker for verse memorization to place on the Sticker Page.)

Prayer

Before class, print the words "Training Plan" in large letters on the top of a sheet of paper and place paper on a clipboard. **What are some ways we can train for God's service?** Write each response on the clipboard. **Let's each choose one way that we plan to train for God's service, and ask Him to help us remember to actually do it!** Lead students in prayer, asking God to help them have the courage to make wise choices. Then give students time to silently ask God for help to follow through on the training plan they chose.

Jeremiah: Prophet in Trouble

Scripture

Bible Story: Jeremiah 36—39
New Testament Connection: Luke 22:39—24:53

Lesson Focus

We can have courage to follow in God's path, even when it is difficult.

Bible Memory Verse

Obey me, and I will be your God and you will be my people. Walk in all the ways I command you, that it may go well with you. Jeremiah 7:23

Optional Enrichment Verse: *This is love: that we walk in obedience to his commands. As you have heard from the beginning, his command is that you walk in love.* 2 John 1:6

Bible Aims

During this session, each student may

1. **DESCRIBE** the ways Jeremiah showed courage by obeying God's commands;
2. **EVALUATE** everyday situations and identify ways to obey God, even when it's hard;
3. **ASK** God to help him or her have courage to obey God in specific situations;
4. **PRAY** to become a member of God's family, as the Holy Spirit leads.

Teacher Devotional

Jeremiah was called from the obscurity of his native town to assume, at a critical hour in the nation's life, the overwhelming responsibilities of a prophet. His father, Hilkiah, was a priest, so Jeremiah inherited the traditions of an illustrious ancestry. His early life was likely also influenced by strong religious leaders. But God had something even better for Jeremiah than to spend his life as a priest serving at the altar. God appointed this young man to be a prophet of the Lord in this trying hour in the history of the chosen people.

Frequently, the Israelites chose to disobey God, even though God's commands had been designed for their well-being. When they stopped following God, they ended up in great trouble. So God warned them through Jeremiah's messages. Just as the people of Israel had to choose whether or not they would listen to the warning in Jeremiah's messages, people today face the choice between following God's ways or pursuing their own ways.

The God of Jeremiah is always ready to give each one of us, and the children we teach, the courage we need to follow in His path, even in difficult circumstances. God's promise of courage springs from His love. He is ready to forgive us when we make a wrong choice, and even better, He is fully able to help us follow Him wholeheartedly so that we can live in the best way possible!

Set the Story 1. (5-10 minutes)

Option A: Hoverboard Hustle

Preparation

If you only have 25 minutes for this center, omit Set the Story. Photocopy and cut out a set of Command Cards for each team. Place each set of cards in a separate pile at one end of the playing area. Make a masking-tape line about 10 to 20 feet (3 to 6 m) from the sets of cards.

Materials Checklist

- ◇ Command Cards (p. 45)
- ◇ scissors or paper cutter
- ◇ 2 skateboards

Optional—

- ◇ 2 10-foot (3-m) lengths of rope

Procedure

Students divide into two teams and line up behind masking-tape line, making sure each team is several feet from the next. Hand a "hoverboard" to first student in each line. Students kneel or sit on hoverboards and use hands to move across the playing area to the card piles. Each student takes a card and then turns around on hoverboard to return to his or her team. (Optional: A volunteer from each team stands next to the team's cards, holding one end of a rope. Stretch the ropes across the playing area to the starting line. Student on hoverboard uses rope to pull himself or herself across the playing area. Student then carries hoverboard back to starting line for the next student.)

The next student in line takes a turn. Beginning with the team that collects all of its cards first, ask team members to select one of the collected cards and then do the command written on the card.

Conversation

Special agents learn to always obey the commands of the agent in charge of a mission. In our game, we obeyed fun commands!

>> **Which of these commands was easy to obey? Why?**

>> **Which command was difficult?**

As special agents in training to serve God, it's important that we know and obey God's commands. Today we're going to hear about a man who needed lots of courage to obey God. We'll find out what he did.

Option B: Around and Around

Preparation

Photocopy and cut out Around and Around Code, making one for each student.

Materials Checklist

- ◇ Bibles
- ◇ Around and Around Code (p. 46)
- ◇ scissors
- ◇ transparent tape

For each student—

- ◇ toilet-paper tube, 5 3/8 inches (13.4 cm) in circumference

Procedure

To solve today's code, you'll need some extra supplies. Allow several minutes for students to figure out the code on their own, using supplies. If after several minutes, students are still having difficulty deciphering the code, lead them to cut their codes into five separate strips. Students tape strips together in numeric order to make one long strip. Students then tape end of first strip to toilet-paper tube. Students wrap the long strip around tube, aligning edges as they go. When done wrapping, students tape end of strip to tube. Ask first student finished to read verse aloud.

Conversation

>> **According to the verse, how do we become God's people?** (By obeying God.)

>> **What does it mean to walk in the ways God has commanded?** (To obey God. To follow God's commands. To do what the Bible says to do.)

>> **What does our verse say will happen if we follow God's commands?** (Things will go well for us. God will help us work things out.)

That doesn't mean that everything will always go smoothly. But it does mean that God is in charge and will be there for us, no matter what happens. Today we're going to talk about having courage to obey God, just like it says in Jeremiah 7:23.

Jeremiah: Prophet in Trouble

Jeremiah 36—39

Preparation

Display Session 4 Bible Story Poster. Use Post-it Notes to mark Jeremiah 36 in students' Bibles. Distribute Bibles to students.

Materials Checklist

- ◇ Session 4 Bible Story Poster from *Elementary Teaching Resources*
- ◇ Post-it Notes

For each student and teacher—

- ◇ Bible

Storytelling Tip

As you tell the story, keep the Daily Mission and the lesson focus in mind. That way, as you tell the story, you will be able to emphasize how the events in the story reinforce the main idea of the session. And through your emphasis, students will more clearly understand and be able to recall the Daily Mission and lesson focus.

Involvement Option

Instead of telling the story as written, dress in Bible-times clothing to portray Jeremiah. Before class, on cards write out questions reporters might ask Jeremiah if he were interviewed about events from today's story. "What did you think when God asked you to write down His words?" "How did you feel when the people didn't listen to God's warning?" "How did you feel when you found out the king had destroyed the scroll?" Number cards in story order and pass out to students. At appropriate times, as you tell a first-person account of the story, signal students to ask the questions and answer as Jeremiah might answer.

Introduction

What's the longest thing you've ever written? How long did it take? Volunteers respond. **Today we're going to hear about a man who wrote an entire book—not once, but twice!** (Optional: Invite students familiar with this story to tell story details. Supplement as needed, referring students to Bible Story Poster for help.)

A Message Revealed

During Bible times, the Israelites had agreed to worship and love the one true God. But people in neighboring countries worshiped a lot of false gods. God didn't want any of HIS people doing such things! But despite what they had agreed to, the Israelites kept turning away from God and doing things their own way—usually following the ways of their neighbors.

God was VERY patient with His people. He sent messengers called prophets to tell them to put God first and to start obeying Him again. These prophets reminded them that God had cared for their ancestors time and time again. The prophets told them that God would always care for them, too. Sometimes after hearing a prophet's message from God the people changed their ways for a little while—but before long they were back to doing wrong things! **Why do you think they acted this way?**

One of these prophets was Jeremiah. Like the other prophets, Jeremiah told the people that doing wrong things would bring BIG trouble. He warned them that God was going to let the Babylonians take them away from their homes. Instead of listening to Jeremiah, the people punished Jeremiah because they didn't like his message! But Jeremiah didn't stop prophesying. He knew God's messages were important.

Read Jeremiah 36:1-3 to find out what God told Jeremiah to do. Jeremiah quickly called for his secretary, Baruch (BEHR-uhk), and dictated to him everything God had said. (In those days, only a few people knew how to read and write.) Once more Jeremiah told God's message that the people would suffer if they didn't start following God. **If you were Jeremiah and Baruch, what would you have done with this book of God's warnings?**

A Message Destroyed

Because Jeremiah's messages had upset and angered so many people, he was no longer allowed to go to the Temple. So Jeremiah sent Baruch to read the finished scroll

aloud in front of everyone. It must have taken a lot of courage for Baruch to deliver this message—after all, he'd seen how much trouble Jeremiah had gotten into! But Baruch stood up in front of the Temple and loudly read God's message.

The message said that if the people didn't start obeying God's commands, the king of Babylon would come and destroy their land. It said that the king would be killed! This time, some people were very interested to hear Jeremiah's message.

There was at least one man in the crowd who understood the seriousness of Jeremiah's message. He ran and found the officials of the country and told them what he'd heard. Well, the officials wanted to hear this message for themselves! So, in secret, they sent for Baruch and asked him to read the scroll aloud.

"This is terrible!" they said. "We have to bring this scroll to the king right away!" The officials hoped the king would listen to the message. But they were afraid he might get angry and want to hurt Baruch and Jeremiah! The officials told Baruch, "You and Jeremiah go and hide. Don't let anyone know where you are!"

The king was sitting by a nice, warm fire in his palace when the officials came to tell him about the scroll. "If you think it's so important, I'll listen to Jeremiah's message," the king may have said.

Read Jeremiah 36:23 to find out how the king reacted when he heard God's message. Even though the officials begged the king not to destroy the scroll, the king did! Then he sent orders out to arrest Jeremiah and Baruch. But because of God's protection, the king's men weren't able to find them.

A Message Repeated

How would you have reacted to the news of this event if you were Jeremiah? How do you think God responded? Read Jeremiah 36:27-28 to find out. It must have taken a lot of patience on Jeremiah's part to rewrite the entire book! But Jeremiah probably thought that if God could be patient, so could he.

Unfortunately, the king didn't listen to Jeremiah this time, either! The people kept doing things that were against God's commands. Eventually, there was a new king. But the new king didn't listen to Jeremiah, either! First, he threw Jeremiah in jail. THEN the king's officials had Jeremiah thrown into a hole deep in the ground where rain water was stored. No one listened to what God told Jeremiah to say. As a sad result, all the terrible things that Jeremiah had told the people would happen DID happen, just like God said they would.

Conclusion

There must have been many times when Jeremiah wanted to give up. But God hadn't given up on the Israelites! So even though it was difficult, Jeremiah kept on following God and telling the people God's message. It isn't always easy for us to obey God, either. But just like Jeremiah, we can have courage to obey God and follow His path, even when it is difficult.

Sometimes when things are difficult or scary, we might find it hard to obey God, too. But if we have courage and ask Him to, He will help us obey and follow in His path. God loves us and wants us to show we love Him by obeying Him!

New Testament Connection

Throughout Jesus' whole life, He always followed in God's path. But in the end, obeying God meant that Jesus would have to allow His enemies to kill him on a cross! Jesus didn't want to die. But in Luke 22:42, Jesus prayed to God saying, "not my will, but yours be done."

Jesus knew that by dying, He could take the punishment for all the wrong things we have done. On the third day after his death, God brought Jesus back to life. Jesus spent some more time teaching His friends how to follow in God's path, and then He went to join God in heaven. Jesus' courage made it possible for us to one day live in heaven, too.

Focus on Evangelism

The greatest and most difficult act of obedience ever was when Jesus died on a cross. Jesus gave His life willingly, because He wanted to obey God and make a way for all of us to become members of God's family. Invite students interested in knowing more about becoming members of God's family to talk with you or another teacher after class. (See "Leading a Child to Christ," p. 8.)

Apply the Story 3.
(10-15 minutes)

Bible Story Review

To review Bible story, students complete "Character Profile" activity on Level 4 page. **What are some of the things that happened to Jeremiah when he told God's messages?** (Arrested. Put in jail. Thrown into a hole with water.) **What risks were Jeremiah and Baruch taking by rewriting the scroll after the king burned it?** (The king would be even more angry. They might have been hurt or killed.) **Why do you think they had the courage to do it anyway?**

Indicate the Daily Mission logo on the page. **Today's Daily Mission is to "FOLLOW in God's Path." What do you think that means?** (To do what God says. To obey God.) **Jeremiah followed in God's path and obeyed God, even when it was hard. Sometimes it isn't easy to follow God's path. But if we ask for His help, God is always willing to give us the courage we need to obey Him.**

Materials Checklist

- ◇ *SFA Manual* Level 4 pages
- ◇ colored markers
- ◇ length of butcher paper

Optional—

- ◇ *SFA Manual* Sticker Pages
- ◇ Daily Missions stickers

Memory Verse/Application

Students turn Level 4 page over. Ask a volunteer to read memory verse aloud. **The Israelites had Jeremiah and the other prophets to remind them about God's commands. But how can WE know what God's commands are?** (By reading the Bible. By listening to our parents and teachers.) **And what are some of those commands?** (Be honest. Don't cheat or steal. Treat others with respect.)

What are some things that can make it HARD for us to obey God's commands? (When we're tired or angry. When we don't know God's commands. When people around us disobey God.) **Why do you think God gave us those commands?** (He loves us and knows what is best for us.) **How do you think following God's commands could help us?** (It helps us avoid situations that could hurt us or others. It helps us do things that we won't regret later.) Students complete "Level 4 Mission" activity. (Optional: Give each student a Daily Missions sticker for verse memorization to place on the Sticker Page.)

Teaching Tip

Tell an age-appropriate example of a time you obeyed God even though it was difficult. Invite students to share their own examples.

Prayer

Roll both ends of a length of butcher paper and attach it to a wall to form a partially opened scroll. **Let's ask God to help us obey His commands.** Brainstorm with students specific situations when it is hard to obey God. Write students' responses on the scroll. Then lead students in prayer, giving time for volunteers to use the responses on the scroll to finish this sentence prayer: "Dear God, please give us courage and help us to obey You when . . ."

Joshua: Spy in a Strange Land

Scripture

Bible Story: Numbers 13—14:9
New Testament Connection: Matthew 28:18-20

Lesson Focus

We can have courage to lead others to God's promises.

Bible Memory Verse

Be strong and courageous. Do not be terrified; do not be discouraged, for the Lord your God will be with you wherever you go. Joshua 1:9
Optional Enrichment Verse: *Always be prepared to give an answer to everyone who asks you to give the reason for the hope that you have.* 1 Peter 3:15

Bible Aims

During this session, each student may

1. **DESCRIBE** how Joshua and Caleb had courage to believe in God's promises and to tell others about them;
2. **DISCOVER** some of the promises that God has given us in the Bible, and discuss ways kids can help others to believe in them;
3. **THANK** God for His promises, and ask God for courage to help others believe in His promises;
4. **PRAY** to become a member of God's family, as the Holy Spirit leads.

Teacher Devotional

The book of Joshua provides a wealth of encouragement and wisdom for the followers of God. Yet this book is not only about following God but also about leading others to Him. As we follow the story of Joshua, we see a man who is determined to trust God's promises and equally determined to lead His people to receive those promises.

Picture this scene: The children of Israel have recently been freed from slavery in Egypt and are on the verge of inheriting the Promised Land. But, because of their fear, the poor Israelites are ready to turn back to the slavery they have just left behind. They cannot invade this land filled with "giants" and take the walled cities. The conquest of the land seems impossible!

Now, Caleb and Joshua had seen the same "giants" and had inspected the same fortifications, yet they insisted that the land could be taken! Because of their courage and trust in God's promises, they were ready to LEAD these people.

God sometimes calls us to lead others in fearful situations, too. When He does, we have the same words that were given to Joshua in answer to his prayer for help in his great undertaking: *Be strong and courageous. Do not be terrified; do not be discouraged, for the Lord your God will be with you wherever you go* (Joshua 1:9). These words are just as true for us!

Option A: Promise Plates

Preparation

If you only have 25 minutes for this center, omit Set the Story. Make a photocopy of the Promise Cards on page 47. Cut cards apart and tape each card to the bottom of a separate paper plate. Place plates facedown in a pyramid pattern on the floor. Make a masking-tape starting line about 10 feet (3 m) from the plates.

Materials Checklist

- ◇ Promise Cards (p. 47)
- ◇ scissors
- ◇ paper plates
- ◇ masking tape
- ◇ beanbag

Procedure

Students take turns tossing the beanbag at the paper plates. If the beanbag lands on a plate, the student who tossed the beanbag turns the plate over and reads the promise written on it. When all plates have been turned over, mix them up and lay them facedown on the floor and start again. Continue until each student has had at least one turn or as time allows. For added challenge, vary the way that students throw beanbag (eyes closed, over the shoulder, under a leg, etc.).

Conversation

Playing our game has revealed several of God's promises to us. These promises come from God's Word, the Bible.

>> **Which of these promises is your favorite? Why?**

>> **When is a time one of these promises could help a kid your age?**

Today we're going to hear about two men who believed in God's promises, even when other people didn't.

Option B: Strip Slidin' Away

Preparation

Photocopy and cut out alphabet strips, making one for each student. Photocopy and cut out verse cards, making one for each student. On card stock, photocopy and cut out Alphabet Cards, making one for each student. For each Alphabet Card, cut on lines to make slits. (Optional: Use craft knife to cut slits.)

Materials Checklist

- ◇ Bibles
- ◇ Slidin' Strips and Cards (p. 48)
- ◇ scissors
- ◇ card stock
- ◇ transparent tape
- ◇ pencils

Optional—

- ◇ craft knife and cutting mat

Procedure

Give each student an alphabet strip, a Verse Card and an Alphabet Card. Each student prints his or her name on Alphabet Card. Then he or she threads long alphabet strip through slits on Alphabet Card as shown in sketch.

By sliding the letters on the bottom strip from left to right, we can create our own codes! The top strip of letters stands for the regular letters we use. The bottom strip of letters makes up our code. See if you can discover which letter to place under the letter *A* to decode our verse.

Allow a few minutes for students to experiment. If students haven't discovered that to decode the verse the letter under the *A* on the card needs to be *K*, give them a hint. **Find the word "kxn" in our coded message. This stands for a word we use to put two things together. What might this word be?** If students are still having difficulty, tell them, **Move the bottom strip so that the letter *K* is under the *A*. Now, write the letter from the card that lines up on top of the letter from our code on the blank lines.**

Conversation

Using our decoder helped us crack our special-agent code and discover today's memory verse from the Bible.

>> **What does God command us to be in today's verse?** (Strong and courageous.)

>> **When are some times it might be hard to be strong and courageous?** (When friends want me to do something wrong. When something bad has happened.)

>> **What promise does God give in this verse to help us be strong and courageous?** (God promises to always be with us.)

Today we're going to talk about ways we can have courage, as Joshua 1:9 says, and ways to help others learn about God's promises.

2. Tell the Story (10 minutes)

Joshua: Spy in a Strange Land

Numbers 13—14:9

Preparation

Display Session 5 Bible Story Poster. Use Post-it Notes to mark Numbers 13 in students' Bibles. Distribute Bibles to students.

Materials Checklist

- ◇ Session 5 Bible Story Poster from *Elementary Teaching Resources*
- ◇ Post-it Notes

For each student and teacher—

- ◇ Bible

Storytelling Tip

Know your story well enough to talk with your students rather than read to them. When your eyes are not tied to the words of the story, you are free to focus on the faces of the students in your class. This will both engage the students' attention and minimize disruptions.

Involvement Option

Before class, create signs labeled "Israelites," "Spies" and "Promised Land People." Divide students into three groups. Each group sits together and does a motion when their sign is held up. (For example: Israelites walk in place. Spies hold a hand over their eyes and look from side to side. People in the Promised Land flex their muscles.) Before telling story, practice holding up each sign, with students doing motions. As you tell story, hold up signs at appropriate moments.

Introduction

What are some things in the news recently that make people feel afraid? When the Israelites lived in Egypt, they knew a lot about fear! They had been kept as slaves, forced to work long days doing hard labor. Today we're going to find out what happened when they finally escaped from Egypt. (Optional: Invite students familiar with this story to tell story details. Supplement as needed, referring students to Bible Story Poster for help.)

A Promised Land

God sent Moses to lead the Israelites home to the land that God had given to their ancestor Abraham many years before. Because the Israelites had lived in Egypt for more than 400 years, this generation had never seen their real home. But they'd heard about what a wonderful place it was by listening to the stories of their ancestors. It was called the land of milk and honey.

The Israelites were very eager to escape from Egypt and live in their homeland. But Egypt was the most powerful nation in the world at that time. It was only with God's miraculous help that Moses was able to lead the Israelites out of Egypt, all the way to the Promised Land.

At last the journey was over! Moses told the people they were going to go into the Promised Land and take it as their own. But the people asked Moses to send some spies to check out the place.

A Secret Mission

God agreed to this plan, so Moses selected 12 spies. **What do you think Moses wanted the spies to find out? Read Numbers 13:18-20. What instructions did Moses give to the spies?**

First the spies traveled to the city of Hebron. It was a huge city with large strong walls. And among the people living in Hebron, the spies saw people who were really big and powerful! **How would you have felt if you were the Israelite spies?**

The spies traveled 250 miles (400 km) in 40 days. They saw plenty of food and water. They even cut a cluster of grapes that was so big, two of them had to carry it on a pole! The spies also saw many well-built cities with strong walls around them. With all this information, the spies returned to the Israelites' camp.

The spies reported directly to Moses. Ten of them had this to say: "It IS the land of milk and honey! There's food everywhere. But the people are fierce and powerful! And their cities are huge, with high walls around them!" But two

of the spies—Joshua and Caleb—had a different report. **Read Numbers 13:30 to find out what Caleb said.**

"That would be foolish!" the other 10 spies said. "We couldn't possibly take over that land!" And these 10 spies started telling everyone how dangerous it would be to enter the Promised Land. "The people are HUGE," they said. "They could stomp us out like grasshoppers!"

When the people heard what the 10 spies were saying, they were terrified! They turned against Moses, saying, "We would have been better off dying in Egypt. But you dragged us across a desert so that our children can be slaughtered here! Let's go back to Egypt!" The Israelites had forgotten that God always keeps His promises. **How would remembering God's promises have helped the Israelites?**

Joshua and Caleb were the only spies who believed that God would protect and help the Israelites. But the people would not listen. In fact, they even discussed killing Joshua and Caleb!

A New Plan

God was very angry about that! He had taken good care of His people, helping them to escape from Egypt. He had protected them from danger and made sure that every one of their needs was met. God had never once broken a promise to them. But somehow His people weren't trusting Him to keep his biggest and best promise yet!

Moses knew that God had every right to punish the people for their actions. But He also knew that God loved them, so he asked God to show mercy. **Read Numbers 14:19 to find out what Moses said.** God agreed to forgive the Israelites. But because of their lack of faith, the Israelites would not be able to enter the Promised Land for decades! Instead, they would wander around in the desert. And none of the adults would ever enter the Promised Land—only their children would be able to live there. The only exceptions were Joshua and Caleb, because they had trusted God.

The people of Israel thought only about how scary their situation looked. But Joshua and Caleb had courage because they remembered God's promise to help them. When God finally allowed His people to enter the Promised Land—40 years later!—He chose Joshua and Caleb to lead them.

Conclusion

Joshua and Caleb trusted God and tried to lead others to believe in His promises, too. Like the other spies, they might have been afraid to do what they knew was right. But because they believed God's promises, they had the courage to lead everyone into the Promised Land.

When we're at church, it might seem easy to believe in God and His promises. But when friends want us to do wrong things, it can be hard to do what God wants. That's why God promises to give us courage. And our belief in God can lead others to see that they can believe God and trust in His promises, too.

The Bible is filled with wonderful promises God makes to us. And when we TRUST in God's plans, UNITE with God's people, TRAIN for God's service and FOLLOW in God's path, we can have courage to LEAD others to believe in God's promises, too.

New Testament Connection

In Matthew 28:18-20, Jesus told His disciples to tell people all over the world about God's promises. We call those verses the Great Commission. But Jesus didn't send them out on their own! He promised that He would always be with them. Jesus will always be with us, too. He will help us and give us the strength and courage we need to lead others to God's wonderful promises.

Focus on Evangelism

God's greatest promise is that anyone who asks can become a member of His family. Invite students interested in knowing more about becoming members of God's family to talk with you or another teacher after class. (See "Leading a Child to Christ," p. 8.)

3. Apply the Story (10-15 minutes)

Bible Story Review

To review Bible story, students complete "Character Profile" activity on Level 5 page. **What did all 12 spies see when they went to the Promised Land?** (Plenty of food and water. Huge clusters of grapes. Strong people. Well-built cities with strong walls around them.) **What did the 10 spies focus on when they reported to Moses?** (The strong people and city walls.) **What did Joshua and Caleb have to say?** (They said that the people should trust God and go into the land He had given them.) **Why do you think Caleb and Joshua were so different from the other spies?**

Indicate the Daily Mission logo on the page. **Today's Daily Mission is to "LEAD Others to God's Promises." Knowing God's promises is like being given a wonderful gift. But it's not a gift that we have to keep to ourselves. The way we live our lives can demonstrate to people around us that God's promises are good and He always keeps them! That's one way that we can lead others to believe in God's promises, too.**

Materials Checklist

- ◇ *SFA Manual* Level 5 pages
- ◇ Bible
- ◇ colored markers
- ◇ slips of paper

Optional—

- ◇ *SFA Manual* Sticker Pages
- ◇ Daily Missions stickers

Memory Verse/Application

Students turn Level 5 page over. Ask a volunteer to read memory verse aloud. **God wants us to have courage, but He doesn't expect us to do it on our own! What promise from God do you see in this verse?** (That He will always be with us.) **How does knowing that help us to have courage?** (Because God is powerful. He loves us and will care for us.) **This is only one of many promises in the Bible that help us have courage. Let's find out some of the other promises.** Students complete "Level 5 Mission" activity.

When are some times kids your age need to have courage and believe in God's promises? (When starting middle school or junior high. When taking a test. When performing in a music recital or acting in a play.) **What are some ways you can help kids your age to learn about God's promises?** (Know what God's promises are, and show others that you believe in those promises.) (Optional: Give each student a Daily Missions sticker for verse memorization to place on the Sticker Page.)

Prayer

Tell an age-appropriate example of a time when knowing God's promises helped you. **I'm thankful that I had God's promise to remember. What are some of God's promises that you are thankful for?** Write each response on a separate slip of paper, and tuck it into a Bible. Lead students in prayer, passing Bible around the class. Volunteers remove a slip of paper from the Bible and thank God for the promise listed on the paper. Close prayer by asking God to help you and your students have courage to help others to believe in God's promises.

TOP SECRET
CODE

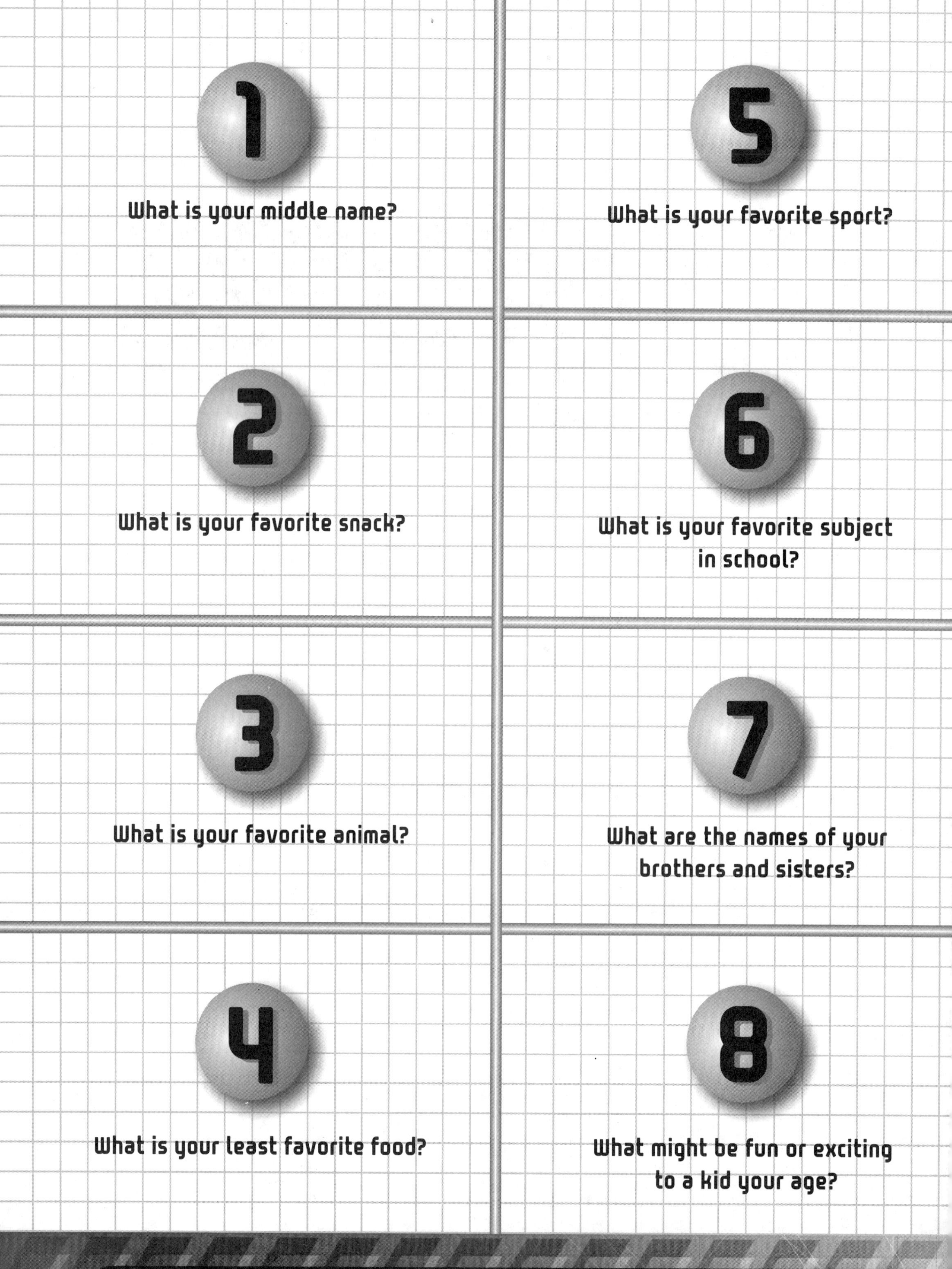
1
What is your middle name?
5
What is your favorite sport?
2
What is your favorite snack?
6
What is your favorite subject in school?
3
What is your favorite animal?
7
What are the names of your brothers and sisters?
4
What is your least favorite food?
8
What might be fun or exciting to a kid your age?

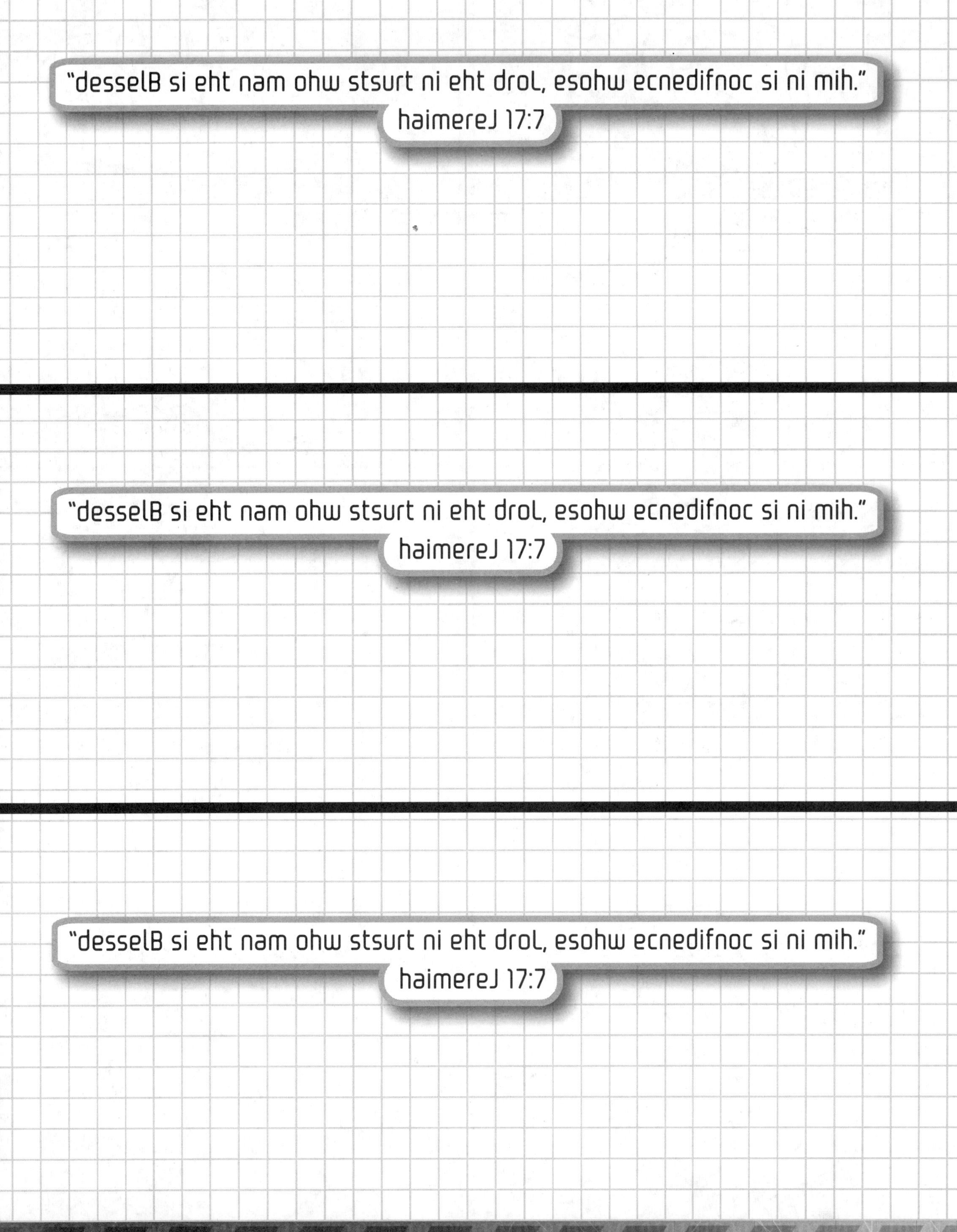

"desselB si eht nam ohw stsurt ni eht droL, esohw ecnedifnoc si ni mih."

haimereJ 17:7

"desselB si eht nam ohw stsurt ni eht droL, esohw ecnedifnoc si ni mih."

haimereJ 17:7

"desselB si eht nam ohw stsurt ni eht droL, esohw ecnedifnoc si ni mih."

haimereJ 17:7

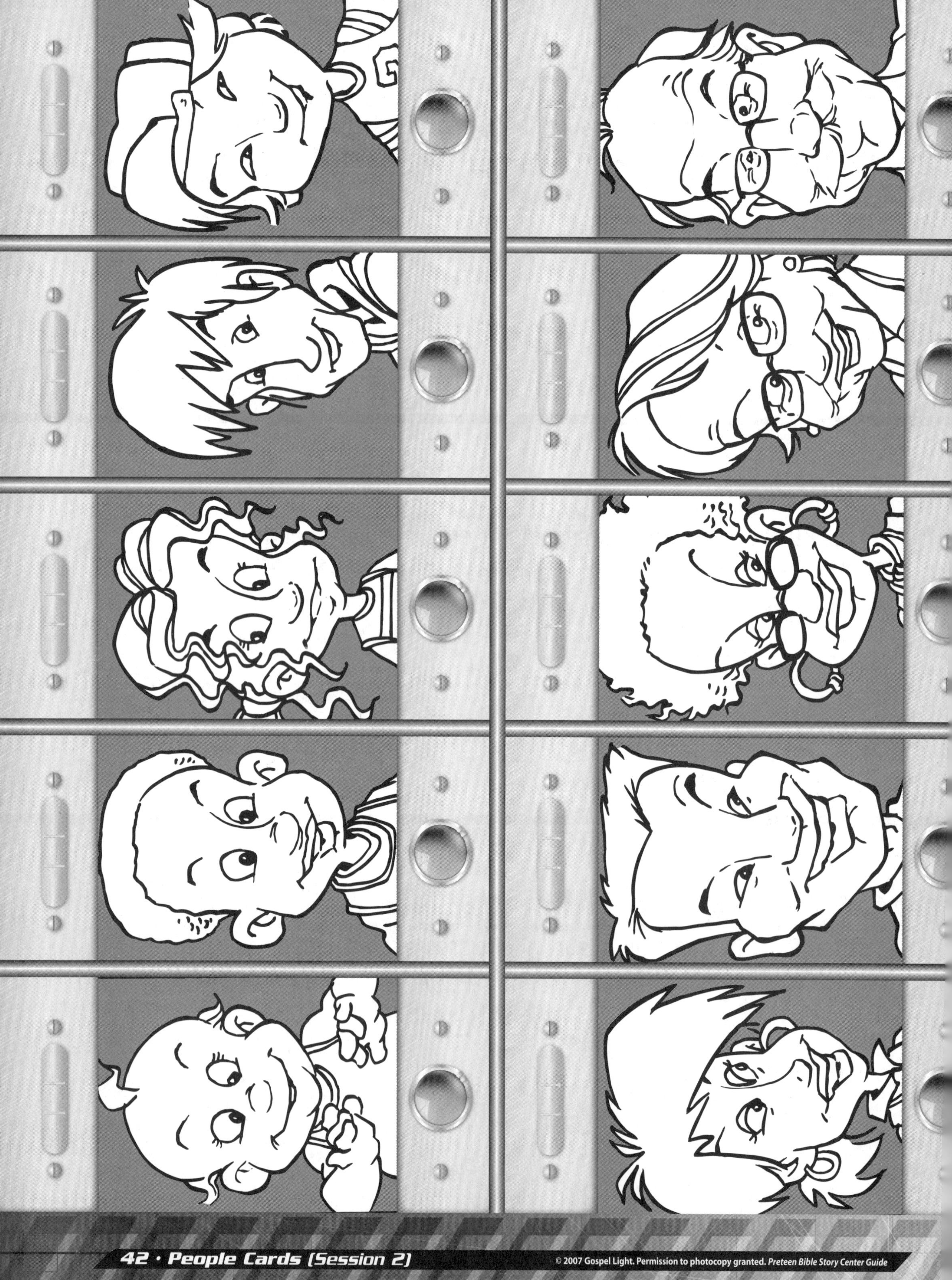

B d v t d o n a o h r n r t e l l v
e e o e t o e n t e i b o h r y o e

H n r n a o h r b v y u s l e R m n 12
o o o e n t e a o e o r e v s o a s 10

B d v t d o n a o h r n r t e l l v
e e o e t o e n t e i b o h r y o e

H n r n a o h r b v y u s l e R m n 12
o o o e n t e a o e o r e v s o a s 10

B d v t d o n a o h r n r t e l l v
e e o e t o e n t e i b o h r y o e

H n r n a o h r b v y u s l e R m n 12
o o o e n t e a o e o r e v s o a s 10

Tic-Tac-Toe Code

A	B	C
D	E	F
G	H	I

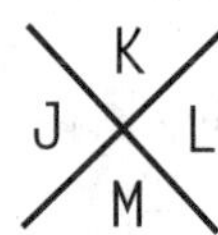

N	O	P
Q	R	S
T	U	V

19:20

Answer Key:

A B C D E F G H I J K L M N O P Q R S T U V W X Y Z

Tic-Tac-Toe Code

A	B	C
D	E	F
G	H	I

N	O	P
Q	R	S
T	U	V

19:20

Answer Key:

A B C D E F G H I J K L M N O P Q R S T U V W X Y Z

Form a pyramid.

Use your bodies to spell the word "love."

Hop up and down on one foot while saying the alphabet.

Count to 10 while spinning around.

Pat your head and rub your belly.

Form a circle and do the "wave."

Close your eyes, tilt your head back and touch the tip of your nose with one finger.

Act like a chicken.

1	2	3	4	5
ll	i	e,		
re	wa	b	yo	
	an	od	23	
	i	ll		
Ob	ma	pe		
I	w	n	an	
yo	mi	ys	e	u.
yo		d	a	
my		t	b	
Wa	ey	y	op	
th	wi	it	al	d
co	ur	ah	I	
th	u		yo	nd
				e
we	lk	m	go	le.
Je	e	ll	h	l
	mm	G	7:	
	at	wi		u,

1	2	3	4	5
ll	i	e,		
re	wa	b	yo	
	an	od	23	
	i	ll		
Ob	ma	pe		
I	w	n	an	
yo	mi	ys	e	u.
yo		d	a	
my		t	b	
Wa	ey	y	op	
th	wi	it	al	d
co	ur	ah	I	
th	u		yo	nd
				e
we	lk	m	go	le.
Je	e	ll	h	l
	mm	G	7:	
	at	wi		u,

1	2	3	4	5
ll	i	e,		
re	wa	b	yo	
	an	od	23	
	i	ll		
Ob	ma	pe		
I	w	n	an	
yo	mi	ys	e	u.
yo		d	a	
my		t	b	
Wa	ey	y	op	
th	wi	it	al	d
co	ur	ah	I	
th	u		yo	nd
				e
we	lk	m	go	le.
Je	e	ll	h	l
	mm	G	7:	
	at	wi		u,

God is with us.

God always loves us.

God hears our prayers.

God gives us courage.

God helps us.

God forgives us.

A B C D E F G H I J K L M N O P Q R S T U V W X Y Z A B C D E F G H I J K L M N O P Q R S T U V W X Y Z

Alphabet Card

Name ______________________

A B C D E F G H I J K L M N O P Q R S T U V W X Y Z

Cut on lines to make slits

Verse Card

Lo cdbyxq kxn myebkqoyec.

Ny xyd lo nscmyebkqon, pyb dro Vybn iyeb

Qyn gsvv lo gsdr iye grobofob iye qy. Tycrek 1:9

....

....

....

....

....